# Praise for Never Meant to Fall

*Never Meant to Fall* is a deeply moving and spiritually grounded memoir that reads like a heartfelt conversation between sisters. J. Renee' invites readers into a vulnerable, honest, and empowering journey of healing, self-discovery, and faith. Through a blend of personal narrative, reflection prompts, humor, and scripture, she crafts a space for women to confront trauma, reclaim their voice, and rise strong.

The book is structured in five parts: Facing the Truth, The Struggle Within, Breaking the Cycle, Rising Strong, and A Legacy of Love, each offering chapters that explore emotional wounds, generational trauma, motherhood, boundaries, forgiveness, and the transformative power of faith. J. Renee's writing is intimate and conversational, often addressing the reader directly as "Sis," which creates a sense of community and shared experience. It's as though she's inviting us to sit with a soft pat on the sofa and a warm "let's talk".

What sets this book apart is its balance of raw honesty and hope. J. Renee' doesn't shy away from the pain of abusive relationships, silent trauma, and the grief of letting go. Yet, she consistently points toward healing, using humor and spiritual insight to guide readers through the darkness.

Her reflections and "Couch Talks" offer practical wisdom and emotional clarity, making the book not only a beautiful memoir but a tool for personal growth.

The affirmations and closing prayer are especially powerful, leaving readers with a sense of peace and purpose. J. Renee's message is clear: you were never meant to fall, you were meant to rise.

Recommended for: Women navigating healing from trauma, faith-based readers seeking encouragement, and anyone looking for a compassionate, empowering voice to walk alongside them on their journey.

Jacqueline Mack-Harris, LMFT, PsyD
Associate Professor, Hope International University


*Never Meant to Fall* is a deeply sentimental, emotionally resonant book that explores themes of self love, healing and redemption.


J. Renee' blends tenderness with straight talk mixed in with a little bit of humor and deep rooted faith. The book offers a chance of reflection within each chapter which really makes the reader look deep within. By the end, you see the life-altering potential of rising through difficulty and trauma into strength and love. -S. Hunter

# NEVER MEANT TO FALL

# NEVER MEANT TO FALL

## TO FALL

### A JOURNEY OF HEALING, LOVE, & RISING STRONG

BY J. RENEE

To my children, who gave me courage when I thought I had none.

And to every sister reading these words, may you find healing, peace, and the strength to rise.

# Acknowledgments

To my family, thank you for loving me through the mess, the mistakes, and the moments I didn't know how to love myself. Your support and unconditional love have been an anchor in my life, and I am forever grateful.

To my sister-friends, you know who you are. Thank you for the late-night talks, the laughter that carried me through heavy days, the prayers when I couldn't find the words, and the reminders that I was never walking alone. You have been my sisters in every way that matters, and I cherish you.

To my therapist, thank you for helping me untangle the knots, peel back the onion, for sitting with me in the hard truths, and for giving me tools to heal when I thought I was beyond repair. Your guidance gave me clarity, your encouragement gave me hope, and your presence gave me strength.

And finally, to every woman who has ever poured into me with a kind word, a prayer, or even just a listening ear, this book is a reflection of not only part of my story, but of the love and support I have been blessed to receive.

# TABLE OF CONTENTS

Introduction-My Dear Sister
A heartfelt invitation into honest, vulnerable, and healing conversations.

## Part One: Facing the Truth

**01** — The Weight of Falling –
*Why we were never meant to fall in love.*

**02** — The Mirror Doesn't Lie –
*The value of being truthful with yourself.*

**03** — The Many Faces of Trauma –
*When pain comes from more than love.*

**04** — The Silent Trauma –
When words cut deeper than bruises.

Couch Talk: Let's Talk About Comparison –
Not measuring your healing against someone else's.

**05** — Red Flags Aren't Green Lights –
Why we convince ourselves we can fix brokenness.

# TABLE OF CONTENTS

# TABLE OF CONTENTS

# TABLE OF CONTENTS

# TABLE OF CONTENTS

# TABLE OF CONTENTS

My Dear Sister,

I've been thinking a lot about life... about love... about what we've been through and what we've overcome. About the moments that left us embarrassed, the choices that made us feel guilty, and the situations that seemed to get the best of us, when all we could do was fight our way through the darkness.

Life comes with so many highs and lows. Some days, we learn the lesson quickly, and other days we're just trying to function, becoming experts at living while depressed. We smile on the outside so the world thinks we're fine, but behind closed doors, all we want to do is bury our face in the pillow and fall apart. We encourage everyone else with, "You'll be okay," while quietly wondering if we ever will.

And then there are the times we've given everything, gone above and beyond for others, while secretly longing for someone to take our hand and whisper, "I've got you."

Sis, that's what this space is for. We're going to walk this journey together. We're going to talk, sit, ride, cry, laugh, and thrive...side by side.

This is for us.

# Part One: Facing the Truth

# Chapter 1

## The Weight of Falling –
## Why We Were Never Meant to Fall in Love

Sis, can I be honest with you?

Growing up, I thought love would come after everything else...after school, after a career, after I was "ready." But instead, I met love too soon, and it pulled me into motherhood, marriage, and decisions that felt right in the moment but left me carrying scars I never imagined. Those choices didn't just shape me, they shaped my children too. They became the beginning of a long road toward healing.

Let me share something with you, that took me years to learn: you were never meant to fall. Falling leaves us bruised, broken, and out of breath. Falling means we've lost balance, lost footing, and often lost sight of ourselves. Falling can feel romantic in the beginning, but it almost always leads to us hitting the ground harder than we ever expected.

When we "fall in love," we tumble headfirst into someone else's world, often leaving our own behind. We ignore the voice inside of us that whispers warnings. We overlook the pieces of ourselves that need tending. And somehow, we convince ourselves that falling is the cost of finding.

But sis, love was never meant to make you fall. Love was always meant to lift.

# The Truth About Falling

Think about it. When you fall, it's sudden. It's unexpected. It takes the wind out of you. That's how so many of us have lived through love...fast, reckless, swept away. And when the dust settles, we're left with the weight of disappointment, shame, or heartbreak pressing heavy on our chest.

And let's be real...some of those "falls" were less like romantic leaps and more like clumsy trips. You ever look back and wonder, "What in the world was I even doing with him?" Sis, if ignoring red flags were a sport, I'd probably have a sponsorship deal by now.

Falling feels like losing control, but rising? Rising feels like reclaiming your place. Rising means standing tall in who you are, grounded in truth, not swayed by every smile, promise, or apology. Rising means love doesn't consume you...it complements you.

## A Sister-to-Sister Reflection

Let me ask you:

- Have you ever mistaken falling for flying? (Whew, I did...thought I was soaring, only to realize I was flat on the ground, eyelashes crooked, dignity gone.)
- Have you ever given so much of yourself away in the name of love that you didn't recognize the woman in the mirror?
- Have you ever told yourself, "If I just hold on a little longer, maybe this will finally feel like love"?

If your heart whispered "yes" to any of those, know that you're not alone. I've been there too, and it nearly broke me.

## What Rising Looks Like

Rising in love is different. It's steady. It's rooted. It doesn't ask you to abandon yourself, it asks you to honor yourself. It doesn't demand silence it, makes space for your voice. It doesn't drain you, it breathes life into you.

Rising love looks like peace, even in the unknown. It looks like joy that isn't borrowed or dependent on someone else's mood. It looks like strength that grows, not fear that shrinks.

And most importantly, rising love begins with you.

## In closing

Sis, I need you to hear me: you were not created to fall in love. Falling was never your story. You were created to rise in love, in truth, in wholeness.

This chapter is the beginning of a shift. From here on, I want us to explore not just what broke us, but what will build us. Not just what made us fall, but what will help us rise.

Because the weight of falling is real...but the freedom of rising is greater.

# Chapter 2

## The Mirror Doesn't Lie –
## The Value of Being Truthful With Yourself

Let's talk about mirrors for a second. Funny thing about them, they don't sugarcoat. They don't play dress-up with your reality. The mirror doesn't care if you're having a good or bad hair day, or if your lashes decided to fight for their independence. It just shows you the truth.

And that's exactly what makes looking at ourselves...really looking...so hard.

For a long time, I couldn't face my own reflection. Not just the one in the bathroom mirror, but the one inside my soul. Because if I stopped long enough to look, I'd have to admit that the woman staring back at me was exhausted, hurting, and pretending she was okay. I'd have to acknowledge the cracks beneath the smile, the truth in my eyes, the pain I thought I was hiding from the world.

Truth is, I wasn't just hiding it from others. I was hiding it from myself.

## Why Honesty With Ourselves Is So Hard

Do you know why we avoid telling ourselves the truth? Because truth demands change. And change is scary. It's much easier to keep saying, "I'm fine" while drowning than to admit, "I'm not okay, and I need help."

We convince ourselves that denial is protection. That if we don't admit the relationship is toxic, then maybe it isn't. That if we pretend our choices aren't hurting us, then maybe they're not.

And here's the kicker, sometimes we get so good at lying to ourselves that we believe it. We'll call pain "strength." We'll call chaos "love." We'll call exhaustion "commitment." Meanwhile, our souls are screaming,

"Sis, stop. Just stop. This is not it."

## A Little Humor in the Hurt

I'll never forget the time I told myself, "This isn't that bad. He just gets angry sometimes." Meanwhile, "angry sometimes" looked like a full-time job with no weekends off. I was out here clocking in for overtime and didn't even realize the pay was in heartbreak.

And if you've ever stood in front of a mirror and practiced the line, "He's not usually like this"... I see you. Been there. Rehearsed it. Sold it like it was gospel truth. The problem is, while I was convincing everyone else, deep down I couldn't convince myself.

Because the mirror doesn't lie.

## Reflection as Liberation

Here's what I've learned: when you finally get honest with yourself, you unlock freedom. It hurts at first, like ripping off a bandage that's been stuck too long...but it's also the only way to heal.

Honesty doesn't make you weak. It makes you whole. When you stand in the mirror and admit, "This isn't working. I'm not happy. I need something different," you give yourself permission to change your story.

## A Sister-to-Sister Reflection

I want you to pause for a moment and ask yourself:

- What truths have I been avoiding?
- Where have I convinced myself red flags are green just to avoid loneliness?
- Am I calling pain "strength" because I'm scared of starting over?

It's okay if the answers sting a little. That sting? That's healing beginning to stir.

## In Closing

Here's the thing, Sis: the mirror will always tell you the truth, whether you're ready or not. But when you stop running from it, when you finally let yourself see the woman staring back at you, flaws, scars, beauty, and all...that's when real freedom begins.

Because the truth doesn't just set you free. It sets you forward.

# Chapter 3

## The Many Faces of Trauma –
## When Pain Comes From More Than Love

When most people hear the word trauma, they think of abuse in relationships. And yes, that is real and damaging. But trauma doesn't just come from partners. It can come from family. It can come from friends. It can even come from strangers or the workplace.

I know, because I have experienced trauma in each of these areas. And let me tell you, it doesn't all feel the same. Depending on who and what caused it, trauma leaves a different kind of mark.

## Family, Friends, and Work

Family trauma cuts in a unique way, because those are the people who were supposed to love and protect us. When that trust is broken, it shakes the foundation of who we are.

Friendship trauma feels like betrayal. These are the people you let into your heart by choice. When that bond is misused or broken, it can make you question your worth and doubt your ability to trust again.

Workplace trauma is often overlooked, but it is real too. When you're mistreated in a place that controls your livelihood, it makes you feel trapped. You go to work every day carrying fear, anxiety, or stress, and it chips away at your confidence and your health.

# Trauma Doesn't Always Show Up Right Away

One of the things I've learned is that trauma doesn't always hit immediately. Sometimes, you can go days, weeks, months, or even years before the weight of it shows up. Your brain has a way of suppressing trauma to protect you. But suppressed pain doesn't stay buried forever.

It often resurfaces in ways you don't expect. Maybe it comes out as fear when you try something new. Maybe it shows up as anger that feels too big for the moment. Sometimes, it doesn't look emotional at all. Sometimes it shows up in your health.

## The Body Remembers

We don't talk enough about how trauma lives in the body. Unprocessed pain can manifest in stress, tension, sleeplessness, and even illness. And I believe one of the most overlooked connections is the link between trauma and auto-immune diseases.

Your body keeps the score. The weight you carried in silence, the pain you swallowed to keep going, the years of holding it together when everything inside you was falling apart, all of that leaves an imprint. Trauma doesn't just shape your mind. It can weaken your immune system, impact your hormones, and create health issues that medicine alone cannot explain.

## Hope in the Awareness

Naming this doesn't mean you are doomed to live under the shadow of trauma forever. What it means is that you can give yourself permission to acknowledge the many faces of trauma. You can stop minimizing your story just because it doesn't look like someone else's.

Pain is pain. Trauma is trauma. And healing is still possible. No matter where it came from. No matter how long ago it happened. No matter how it shows up in your body or in your heart today.

## A Reflection for You

- Where have I experienced trauma outside of romantic love?
- Have I minimized my pain because it didn't "look" like someone else's trauma?
- What signals is my body giving me that I may need to pay attention to?

## In Closing

Trauma has many faces. It can come from the people closest to us, the friends we trusted, the jobs we depended on, and even complete strangers. It can hide for years before surfacing. It can live in your body, your mind, and your spirit.

But here is the truth: naming it is the first step to healing it. You are not weak because it affected you. You are strong because you are facing it now.

And you are not alone.

# Chapter 4

## The Silent Trauma –
## When Words Cut Deeper Than Bruises

Not all trauma leaves visible scars. Some wounds don't show on your skin, but they echo in your mind and linger in your heart. This is the silent trauma, the kind that doesn't leave bruises for others to see, but leaves you questioning your worth, your sanity, and sometimes even your voice.

We don't talk about this kind of trauma enough. Emotional abuse. Verbal attacks. Manipulation. Gaslighting. Words that were meant to cut and control. Because no one sees the marks, people dismiss the pain. But the truth is, sometimes the wounds you cannot see are the hardest to heal.

### When Words Become Weapons

Words can build you up, but they can also break you down. A sentence spoken in anger, a name you were called, or a lie repeated enough times until you believed it, these are wounds too.

Being told "You're nothing," or "No one will ever want you," doesn't leave bruises, but it does leave scars. Being mocked, silenced, or constantly doubted chips away at your confidence until you don't even recognize yourself anymore.

And what makes this trauma so painful is that it often gets minimized. People say, "Well, at least he didn't hit you." As if only broken bones count as proof. But a broken spirit is just as real.

# My Experience With Silent Trauma

I know what it feels like to live with words that pierced deeper than fists ever could. They echoed long after they were spoken. I found myself replaying conversations in my head, wondering if maybe it was my fault, maybe I was too sensitive, maybe I was as worthless as they said.

That is the lie of silent trauma. It convinces you to doubt yourself. It convinces you that because you can't "prove it," it must not be real. But it is real. And it leaves marks that take time, care, and truth to heal.

## The Lingering Effects

Silent trauma doesn't always show up right away. Sometimes the pain resurfaces years later. It comes out as fear, hesitation, anger, or silence. You might hear those old words in your head when you try to step into something new. You might feel yourself shrink in situations where you should be standing tall.

And, as previously stated; the body remembers too. Stress, tension, even illness can be rooted in years of swallowing words that wounded you.

## Humor in the Healing

I remember one time someone tried to insult me with the same tired phrase they had used a hundred times before. And instead of crying, I laughed. Not because it wasn't painful anymore, but because I realized, "That's all you've got? The same old script?" In that moment, I saw clearly that the words said more about them than they ever did about me.

## A Reflection for You

- Have I dismissed my pain because it didn't leave visible scars?

- What words still echo in my mind that I need to release?

- How can I begin speaking truth and love over myself to replace the lies?

## In Closing

Silent trauma is real. It may not leave bruises on your skin, but it leaves bruises on your soul. And those bruises matter.

Healing begins when you stop minimizing the pain and start naming it for what it is. You are not too sensitive. You are not weak. You are not broken beyond repair.

You are beautifully scarred, prayerfully made, and strong enough to rise. Even from the words that tried to silence you.

# Couch Talk: Let's Talk About Comparison

Sis, can we sit on this for a moment? Comparison is one of the sneakiest thieves of joy.

When you're healing, it's easy to look at other women and wonder why their lives look so put together while yours feels like it's falling apart. Social media makes it worse. Everybody's smiling, traveling, or posting about their "perfect" relationship. Meanwhile, you're just trying to get through the day without crying in the bathroom.

Here's the truth: healing doesn't happen on a schedule. And comparison will have you doubting the beautiful work God is already doing in your life.

## The Danger of Looking Sideways

I used to scroll and compare, thinking, "She looks so happy. She must not have gone through what I did. She's stronger than me." But I learned something important — people only show you what they want you to see. Behind every highlight reel is a real story, and you don't know what someone had to walk through to get to where they are.

And honestly? Half the time, they're struggling too.

## Your Journey is Yours

No two healing journeys look alike. Some women take bold steps fast. Others move slower and more quietly. Neither is wrong. The point isn't speed, the point is that you're moving forward.

Your healing is not late. Your rising is not delayed. You are right on time for your story.

## Reflection for You

- Do I find myself comparing my healing to someone else's journey?
- What lies do I believe about myself when I look at others?
- How can I celebrate my own progress without needing it to look like anyone else's?

## In Closing

Comparison will always steal your joy if you let it. But when you focus on your lane, your healing, and your God, you will see that you are exactly where you need to be.

Your journey is not supposed to look like hers. It's supposed to look like yours.

# Chapter 5

### Red Flags Aren't Green Lights –
### Why We Convince Ourselves We Can Fix Brokenness

Have you ever looked back on a relationship and thought, "Wow, all the signs were there. I just decided to ignore them like they were on sale at a clearance rack"?

Red flags aren't subtle. They wave, they flap in the wind, sometimes they smack us right in the face. And yet, so many of us find ourselves treating them like little decorations instead of the warnings they are. We turn them green in our minds, convincing ourselves, "It's not that bad… maybe I can fix it… maybe he'll change."

The truth is, most of us aren't blind to red flags. We're just experts at justifying them.

## Why We Ignore the Obvious

There are so many reasons we paint red flags green:

- Hope: We want to believe in the best version of someone, even if they're not showing up that way.
- Fear: The thought of being alone feels heavier than the reality of being mistreated.
- Pride: We don't want to admit we made the wrong choice, so we keep doubling down.
- Love: Or at least what we think is love — but really it's attachment, habit, or the fantasy of what could be.

And sometimes, let's be real, we confuse being needed with being valued. We think, "If I just love him harder, maybe he'll love me better." That mindset will wear you out faster than a pair of cheap heels on a rainy day.

## My Own Red Flags

I remember being in a relationship where the red flags weren't just waving, they were practically neon lights with sirens attached. Anger issues, manipulation, habitual lying, constant excuses… and still, I told myself, "But he says he loves me."

It's amazing what you'll accept when you're desperate to feel chosen.

I wish I could say I saw the truth right away, but no. I convinced myself his "bad days" were just stress. That if I could be patient, supportive, forgiving...maybe I could turn him into the man I needed him to be.

But here's the reality: love can encourage growth, but it cannot be a construction project. You are not Home Depot, and he is not your weekend fixer-upper.

## Even Healthy Love Takes Work

Let me pause and say this: even the healthiest relationships take work. No love story is perfect. You still have to nurture it, show up daily, and grow through challenges together. But there's a difference between the work that builds and the work that breaks.

In an unhealthy relationship, you're not just working on communication or understanding. You're working on survival. You're patching holes in a sinking ship while trying to convince yourself it's still worth sailing. You're working on your own breaking, all because you believed the lie that if you just held on tighter, prayed harder, or loved deeper, you could change a man who had no intention of changing.

And here's the truth we don't like to say out loud: you cannot rebuild someone who refuses to rebuild themselves.

## Humor in Hindsight

If I'm honest, I sometimes laugh at the things I excused. Like how "He just needs time to change" turned into "He just needs a whole personality transplant." Or how I prayed, "Lord, help him grow," when what I really needed was to pray, "Lord, help me go."

There's humor in hindsight, but back then it was anything but funny. It was painful. It cost me peace, self-respect, and years of my life.

## A Reflection for You

Take a moment and ask yourself:

- What red flags have I convinced myself were just "quirks"?
- Am I calling dysfunction "commitment"?
- Where have I taken on the role of "fixer" when I was never meant to be anyone's savior?

Being honest with yourself about the red flags isn't about judgment — it's about freedom. The moment you stop painting them green, you open the door to a love that doesn't drain you, but sustains you.

## In Closing

Red flags will always exist, but the question is: will you stop at the warning or will you speed right through it? Choosing to stop, to pause, to see things as they are, that's where your power begins.

Because love is not about fixing someone else. Love is about choosing someone who's willing to grow alongside you. And more importantly, love is about choosing yourself enough to walk away when those flags wave high.

# Chapter 6

The Myth of Superwoman –
Why carrying everything on your back isn't strength,
and how to lay the weight down.

We've all heard it: "You're so strong."
And at first, it sounds like a compliment. It feels like validation. But after a while, those words start to feel like chains. Because what people are really saying is, "I see your struggle, and I expect you to keep carrying it."

Somewhere along the way, many of us bought into the myth of Superwoman. The woman who does it all, holds it all, fixes it all — without breaking a sweat. She's the mom, the partner, the friend, the worker, the fixer, the peacemaker, the prayer warrior, the one everyone calls when their world falls apart. And she shows up smiling, even while she's crumbling inside.

## The Cost of the Cape

The cape looks good from the outside. But wearing it comes at a cost. Behind the mask of strength is exhaustion. Behind the smile is resentment. Behind the "I got this" is a silent scream: "Who's going to carry me?"

I lived that life, saying yes when I wanted to say no, solving problems that weren't mine, pouring out of a cup that was already empty. And do you know what it gave me? Sleepless nights, headaches, resentment, and a heart that was running on fumes.

Strength isn't about never breaking down. True strength is knowing when to put the cape down.

## Humor in the Myth

I remember one week where I thought I could do it all: work, cook, clean, take care of the kids, volunteer, and still be a loving partner. By Friday, I was sitting on the couch surrounded by unfolded laundry, eating A small pack of donuts, and thinking, "So this is what Superwoman eats for dinner."

Sometimes you have to laugh at yourself, because the myth of Superwoman is just that... a myth. Nobody can do it all without breaking.

## A Reflection for You

- Where in my life am I pretending to be "Superwoman" when I'm really just exhausted?
- Do I believe that asking for help makes me weak?
- What cape do I need to take off so I can finally breathe?

## In Closing

The myth of Superwoman tells us that strength is carrying it all. But real strength is knowing what's yours to carry and what's not. It's setting the cape down and saying, "I am human. I am worthy of rest. And I don't have to do this alone."

Because love, healing, and rising are not about how much weight you can carry...they're about how much space you can create for peace, joy, and freedom.

# Part Two:
# The Struggle Within

# Chapter 7

## When Control Masquerades as Love – Untangling Manipulation, Fear, and False Strength

There's a thin line between being loved and being managed. And for a long time, I didn't know the difference.

Control doesn't always show up as chains or loud demands. Sometimes it sneaks in disguised as "care." It sounds like, "I just don't want you to wear that." Or, "Don't talk to him, I don't trust his intentions." At first, it feels flattering, like someone loves you enough to be protective. But over time, protection turns into possession. And what once felt like care begins to feel like a cage.

## Why Control Feels Like Love

It's easy to mistake control for love because, in the beginning, it can look like attentiveness. Someone checking in on where you are, who you're with, how you're spending your time...it can feel like, "Wow, he really cares."

But here's the truth: love supports, while control suffocates. Love celebrates your freedom, while control monitors it. Love says, "I trust you." Control says, "I own you."

And sometimes, we welcome that control because it makes us feel chosen, wanted, or even safe. But that safety is an illusion, and the cost of it is your peace, your voice, and sometimes even your identity.

## My Experience With Control

I remember a time when I couldn't make the simplest decisions without checking in, what to wear, can I go out with my friends, even what job to take. I thought it was "partnership." In reality, it was me slowly shrinking, trading my independence for approval.

And here's the part I laugh about now but couldn't then: I once got accused of "taking too long" at the grocery store. Sis, it was a twenty-minute run, and he was convinced I was living a double life in aisle seven. At the time, it crushed me. Now? I shake my head at the thought of being interrogated over milk and bread.

## Control Disguised as Strength

Many controllers pride themselves on being "strong" or "leaders." They use words like "I just know what's best" or "I'm trying to guide us." But leadership without respect is just manipulation in a nice suit.

Here's what I've learned: someone who truly loves you doesn't want to be the only strong one in the room. They want to stand strong with you, not over you. They want to empower you, not diminish you.

## A Reflection for You

Take a moment and ask yourself:

- Has someone's "care" started to feel more like control?
- Do you feel like you need permission to be yourself?
- Have you confused restriction with protection?

It's not love if you have to shrink yourself to keep it alive.

## In Closing

Control masquerading as love is one of the most dangerous disguises because it convinces you that captivity is care. But real love? Real love never clips your wings. It doesn't ask you to shrink, it helps you expand. It doesn't bind you, it builds you.

The day you learn the difference is the day you stop confusing possession with passion, and start recognizing that love was never meant to control you. It was meant to see you, celebrate you, and rise with you.

# Chapter 8

## The Grief of Strength –
## Why Letting Go Feels Like Mourning

People love to praise strength. "You're so strong." "I don't know how you do it." "You'll get through this." And yes, strength is powerful, but what they don't tell you is that sometimes strength feels like grief.

Because strength often means letting go. And letting go feels like a funeral without flowers.

## Why Letting Go Hurts So Much

Letting go doesn't just mean walking away from a person. It can mean releasing an old version of yourself, a dream that never came true, or a hope you held onto so tightly it left marks on your hands.

We grieve not only the love we lost, but also the love we thought we'd have. We grieve the future we imagined, the wedding anniversaries, the family dinners, the "one day it'll all work out." Letting go asks us to bury not just the relationship, but the fantasy too.

And that kind of grief is heavy. It's not always dramatic; sometimes it's quiet. Sometimes it's sitting in your car in the grocery store parking lot, crying because you realized you no longer have to call and check in, and that silence feels like both freedom and loss.

## The Strength We Don't Talk About

The world claps for strength that looks like holding on. But the real applause should be for the strength it takes to walk away. To admit, "This isn't good for me." To choose peace over chaos, even when chaos is familiar.

It's funny how we'll say, "She's so strong, she stayed through everything," when the truth is, it often takes far more strength to leave. Staying doesn't always make you strong, sometimes it just makes you stuck.

And I'll be honest: when I finally let go, I didn't feel strong. I felt broken. I also questioned myself continuously, second guessing whether I had made the right choice. But strength doesn't always roar. Sometimes strength whispers, "I can't keep doing this. I deserve better."

## A Little Humor in the Healing

I remember the day I started packing. I had planned it a couple of weeks before I even began, because I knew that if he saw I was packing, it would be a problem... a serious problem. This time I was careful, and I had thought the process out. Because I had left before and returned, I knew it could not go the same way again. I packed up and quietly took our belongings out every other night, moving them to my parents' house. There was no way I could take everything I desired, because I knew he wouldn't allow it. I remember our son asking, "Mom, why can't I take my Xbox?" And I had to tell him, "If we take your Xbox, your dad will notice we're not coming back." As the time came closer to the date we left, I was going through not only my clothes and belongings, but the kids' too, thinking to myself, "I'd rather just start from scratch."

It's strange how we attach ourselves to the smallest things, a hoodie, a scent, a song, like they're proof of love. And then one day you realize you don't miss the person, you just miss the routine. That realization hits different, and it makes you laugh and cry at the same time.

## A Reflection for You

If you've ever had to let go, ask yourself:

- Am I grieving the person, or the fantasy of what I hoped we'd be?
- Have I confused staying with strength?
- What could open up in my life if I shifted my strength from holding on to moving forward?

## In Closing

Strength and grief are often twins. You can't have one without the other. But here's the beauty: every time you let go of something that was breaking you, you create space for something that will build you.

So if you feel like you're mourning while you're moving forward, know this: that grief is proof that you were brave enough to release what was unworthy of you. And that kind of strength is sacred.

Because sometimes the strongest thing you can do is not to hold on, but to let go.

# Chapter 9

## Afraid of Joy –
## How Pain Teaches Us to Fear Happiness and Love

It's a strange thing when happiness makes you nervous. When laughter feels suspicious. When joy feels like a setup, like the calm before the storm.

If you've ever caught yourself waiting for the other shoe to drop every time life finally feels good, you know exactly what I mean. It's like trauma rewires your brain to believe joy isn't safe. You start thinking, "If I get too happy, something bad will happen. If I let myself love this moment, it won't last."

That's what pain does, it teaches us to mistrust the very things our souls were created to enjoy.

## Why We Fear Joy

There are a few reasons this happens:

- We've been blindsided before. When you've been knocked down out of nowhere, joy feels like a trick.
- We don't trust good things. We get so used to chaos that peace feels foreign.
- We equate joy with vulnerability. If I let myself feel happy, I risk being hurt when it's gone.

And let's be real, sometimes joy feels like standing on a stage in a brand-new dress, just waiting for someone to point out a stain you didn't know was there.

## My Struggle With Joy

After leaving my past relationships, I thought freedom alone would bring happiness. And in some ways it did — but it also came with its own shadows.

I'd have moments of joy with my kids, laughing in the living room or having a small party in my Parents backyard, and then this wave of guilt would hit me: "Why didn't I give them this sooner? Why did they have to go through all of that first?"

And instead of letting joy wash over me, I'd push it away. I didn't realize it at the time, but I was afraid of joy. Afraid to believe we deserved it. Afraid that if I let myself fully embrace it, it would slip through my fingers.

## Humor in the Healing

I remember one time I went over to a close sister-friend's house and ended up staying the night. We talked, cried, and laughed together, the kind of soul-nourishing time that reminds you what real connection feels like. And then suddenly, I caught myself thinking, "I need to leave before I get in trouble."

That's when it hit me: I was free.

Driving back home that morning, I cried, I thanked God, and I laughed all at once. For the first time in a long time, I realized I could experience relationships that brought me joy without the shadow of punishment hanging over me. I was free to love, free to laugh, free to stay the night at a friend's house and not have to explain myself to someone who wanted to control me.

Looking back, I laugh at myself, but in the moment it was real. That's how deeply pain can condition us, to expect disaster even in the middle of our blessings.

## Choosing Joy Anyway

Here's what I've learned: joy is not the absence of pain, it's the refusal to let pain have the final word.

Joy is risky, yes. It makes you vulnerable. But vulnerability is not weakness, it's the doorway to healing. When you choose joy, you're choosing to tell your past, "You don't get to steal this from me anymore."

And the beautiful thing is, joy doesn't have to be loud or extravagant. Sometimes it's as simple as peace in your heart, laughter with your children, or a moment of stillness where you realize, "I made it through."

## A Reflection for You

- Do I sabotage moments of joy because I'm afraid they won't last?
- Am I holding guilt or shame that keeps me from receiving happiness?
- What would it look like to let myself enjoy good moments without fear of the future?

## In Closing

Joy isn't fragile, it's resilient. It doesn't mean bad things won't happen again, but it reminds you that good things still can.

So don't be afraid of joy. Don't side-eye it. Don't push it away. Embrace it, dance in it, laugh inside of it. Because every time you let yourself feel joy, you're telling the world, and yourself, that healing has the final say.

# Couch Talk: Let's Talk About Trust

Trust is one of the hardest things to rebuild after you've been hurt. And I'm not just talking about trusting other people. Sometimes the hardest person to trust again is yourself.

When I looked back at some of the choices I made, I caught myself thinking, "How did I not see it? Why did I let that happen? How could I have ignored the signs?" And that shame made me second-guess my own voice.

Here's the truth, sis: trauma teaches you to doubt yourself. But healing teaches you to trust yourself again.

## Trusting Yourself Again

It doesn't happen overnight. At first, I had to start small. I learned to trust myself in little things. Choosing what I wanted to eat without asking someone else first, deciding how to spend a day, or saying no when I was used to saying yes.

Those small choices reminded me that I could hear my own voice again, and more importantly, that I could follow it.

## Trusting Others, Slowly

Trusting others came later. And I learned that trust doesn't mean blind faith. Trust means watching for consistency, listening to actions more than words, and honoring your boundaries even when people push against them.

And guess what? It's okay to take your time. Trust built slowly is stronger than trust given too quickly.

## Reflection for You

- Do I struggle more with trusting myself, or with trusting others?

- What small choices can I make today to rebuild my trust in my own voice?

- Who in my life has shown consistency that is worthy of trust?

## In Closing

Trust is not about being naïve. It's about being wise. It's about learning to hear your own voice, honoring it, and giving trust to others who have proven they can handle it.

And most importantly, it's about remembering that God can be trusted above all else, even when people fail.

# Chapter 10

On Forgiving Yourself –
Breaking the cycle of guilt and shame.

We talk a lot about forgiving others. Forgiving the ones who hurt us. Forgiving the ones who broke promises. Forgiving the ones who left scars. But do you know what's even harder sometimes? Forgiving yourself.

For years, I carried guilt like it was a backpack I couldn't take off. Guilt for staying too long. Guilt for going back. Guilt for the nights my kids saw more than they should have. Guilt for not leaving sooner, for choosing wrong, for not protecting myself the way I thought I should have.

And here's the thing, no one had to remind me. I was my own accuser. I replayed every mistake in my mind on repeat, like a bad movie I couldn't turn off.

## Why We Struggle to Forgive Ourselves

Forgiving yourself feels impossible because it forces you to face the truth: that you're human. And sometimes being human means making choices that were rooted in survival, fear, or hope that things would be different.

We think if we punish ourselves long enough, we'll somehow "make up" for the past. But guilt doesn't heal you, it chains you. Shame doesn't make you stronger, it just keeps you small.

## My Own Journey with Self-Forgiveness

I remember looking at my children one day and feeling overwhelmed with shame. I thought, "They deserved better than what I gave them. I failed them." It crushed me.

But over time, I realized something: I couldn't go back and rewrite the past. All I could do was write a better future. My kids didn't need me to be perfect, they needed me to be present, healing, and willing to rise. And to do that, I had to forgive myself for the choices I made when I didn't know better.

## Humor in the Healing

Self-forgiveness doesn't happen overnight. I used to joke that I wished God had a "delete history" button like the one on my computer. One click and poof, every bad choice gone. But life doesn't work like that. Instead, God gives us grace. Grace to learn, grace to heal, grace to move forward even with the past still behind us.

## A Reflection for You

- What guilt have I been carrying that no one else is holding over me anymore?
- Do I believe God's grace is big enough to cover even my mistakes?
- What would change in my life if I treated myself with the same compassion I give others?

## In Closing

Forgiving yourself doesn't mean you excuse what happened. It means you refuse to let shame own you. It means you honor the woman you are today instead of punishing the girl you once were.

Because the truth is, you did the best you could with what you knew at the time. And now that you know better, you can live better. That's not failure, that's growth.

# Part Three:
# Breaking the Cycle

# Chapter 11

## Scars Tell the Story –
## My Journey Through Abuse, Loss, and Survival

Scars are strange things. At first, they're tender reminders of pain, the wound you thought might never heal. But over time, scars stop being open wounds and start becoming proof. Proof that you survived. Proof that what tried to break you didn't win. Proof that there's life after pain.

I carry scars that no one can see. They're not on my skin, but in my soul. They live in the memories I tried to bury, in the nights I cried myself to sleep, and in the mornings I woke up determined to pretend everything was fine.

### The First Marriage

I married young, right as I was stepping into motherhood for the first time. I thought love meant enduring whatever came. I thought if I fought back, if I showed I was strong, then the abuse wasn't "that bad." But abuse doesn't become less damaging just because you swing back.

The abuse wasn't only physical. It was mental, emotional, financial, and verbal. And while I was trying to survive, I didn't realize how deeply my daughter was being affected, watching her mother endure violence, confusion, and fear. Those scars weren't mine alone. They marked her too.

## Spinning the Block

When I finally escaped, I didn't pause to heal. I didn't take time to breathe, to rebuild, or to give my child the stillness she needed. Instead, I did what so many of us do, I "spun the block" and went back to someone from my past.

At first, it felt like redemption, like maybe this time would be different. But the truth revealed itself slowly, in years of devaluing, manipulation, and more abuse. Children came into the picture, and with them, more lives were tied to the chaos.

Looking back, I see now that I was infected, not with something physical, but with rejection, self-doubt, and a twisted version of love that told me abuse was normal if it came with apologies, and if I fought back.

## The Breaking Point

Living in those conditions pushed me to make decisions that I thought were best for my children and me, but in reality, they were choices made from survival, not wisdom. And survival can only take you so far before it cracks you open.

There came a point when the layers began to peel back, and everything unraveled. The truth could no longer be hidden... not from me, and not from my kids. That unraveling was terrifying. But it was also necessary. Because only when the truth comes out can healing begin.

## Humor in the Hurt

I'll be honest, there are parts I can look back on now and laugh, not because they were funny, but because I can't believe what I accepted. I think about the times I rehearsed excuses like I was auditioning for a role: "He's just under stress... he didn't mean it... it was my fault." I deserved an Oscar for some of the performances I gave, trying to convince the world, and myself, that we were okay.

But deep down, I knew better. And my scars remind me of that.

## Why I Share This Story

I don't share any of this for pity. I share it because scars tell the truth. They remind us where we've been, but they also show us how far we've come. My scars are not signs of weakness, they are evidence of survival. They are markers of strength. They are proof that even in the darkest places, light can find its way in.

## A Reflection for You

- What scars are you carrying that you try to hide?
- Do you see them as shameful reminders, or as proof that you survived?
- What story could your scars tell if you allowed them to speak healing instead of hurt?

## In Closing

My story is not neat. It's not polished, but it's mine. And while I would never have chosen the pain, I can say now that the scars it left behind became part of my testimony.

Scars are not the end of the story. They are the evidence that the story is still being written. And every time I see mine, I'm reminded: I am still here. I survived. And I am rising.

# Chapter 12

## Unraveling the Onion –
## What Happens When the Layers of
## Hurt Are Peeled Back

Healing isn't a one-and-done process. It's not a straight line, it's not pretty, and it definitely doesn't happen overnight. Healing is more like peeling an onion, one layer at a time. And if you've ever cut into an onion, you know what happens: the tears come whether you want them to or not.

That's how healing works. You start peeling back the layers of your life, the pain, the trauma, the patterns, and the many coats you had to put on just to endure what you were experiencing. Suddenly you're crying over things you thought you were "done with."

## The Layers We Hide Behind

Some of the layers are easy to name: heartbreak, betrayal, loss. But others are hidden beneath those first layers; rejection, shame, abandonment, fear. They stack up over the years, and we build our identities around them without even realizing it.

I remember thinking I was "strong" because I could carry it all. But in reality, I was just covered in layers that kept me from breathing. It wasn't strength, it was survival. And survival doesn't give you peace, it just keeps you alive long enough to realize you need healing.

## When the Tears Surprise You

The hardest part about peeling back layers is that sometimes the tears catch you off guard. You'll be doing fine, moving forward, and then one song, one scent, one memory comes back, and suddenly you're back in that moment of pain.

I can't tell you how many times I thought I was "over it" only to find myself crying in the car, asking God, "Why does this still hurt?" That's when I realized healing isn't about getting rid of every tear, it's about letting the tears wash through you without drowning in them.

## Humor in the Mess

And let's be real, some layers of healing are just plain messy. Like the time I thought I was having a "spiritual breakthrough" because I stayed calm during an argument, only to lose it the next day because someone ate the last slice of cheesecake. Healing will humble you like that.

Sometimes we laugh not because it's funny, but because if we don't, we'll stay stuck in the heaviness. And laughter itself becomes a layer of healing too.

## The Gift of the Layers

Here's the thing: peeling hurts, but every layer you shed makes you lighter. You begin to uncover the real you beneath all the pain, the you who still believes in joy, the you who can trust again, the you who can stand in front of a mirror and see not just scars, but strength.

The layers don't disappear overnight. But each one you peel back brings you closer to wholeness.

A Reflection for You

- What layers am I still carrying that I pretend don't exist?
- Where have I mistaken survival for true healing?
- Can I allow myself to cry without feeling ashamed of the tears?

## In Closing

Healing isn't about rushing to the end. It's about giving yourself permission to peel back one layer at a time, even if it stings, even if it makes you cry.

Because on the other side of every tear is a little more light, a little more freedom, and a little more of the woman you were always meant to be.

# Chapter 13

## Healing in the Light – Choosing Self-Care, Truth, and Faith

There comes a point in the healing journey when you realize you can't stay in the shadows forever. Yes, the shadows feel familiar. Yes, they even feel safe because you've grown used to them. But shadows keep you surviving. Light helps you live.

Healing in the light means making a choice, to show up for yourself, to walk in truth, and to believe that God's love is big enough to hold your story.

## Self-Care Beyond the Surface

We live in a world that sells self-care as bubble baths and candles. And while I love a good soak in the tub, real self-care goes deeper than that. Real self-care is setting boundaries even when it disappoints people. It's resting without guilt. It's telling yourself "no" when you're about to chase the same old cycle again.

For me, self-care meant giving myself permission to stop pretending. To stop smiling for everyone else while I was collapsing inside. It meant choosing health over hustle, peace over pretending, and wholeness over appearances.

## Truth as Medicine

Healing in the light also means being anchored in truth. And truth is not always pretty. Sometimes it's uncomfortable, sometimes it's humbling. But truth is the only soil where healing can grow.

I had to stop telling myself stories like, "He'll change if I love him enough." Or, "This is just how life is for me." Those lies were shadows. The truth, even when it stung, was light.

And here's the thing about truth: it doesn't just expose, it heals. The same way a wound has to be cleaned out before it can close, your heart has to be honest before it can truly heal.

## Faith as Foundation

Through it all, my faith carried me. There were nights I was angry at God, mornings I questioned why He allowed me to walk through so much pain. But even in my questions, His presence was constant.

I prayed for escape, and God made a way. I prayed for strength, and even when I felt weak, He gave me enough to take the next step. Faith didn't erase my scars, but it gave my scars meaning. It reminded me that my story didn't end with brokenness.

## Humor in the Light

And can I be real? Sometimes healing in the light looks like laughing at yourself. Like the time I decided to "rest in God's peace" but ended up binge-watching a whole season of a show instead. I told myself it was "self-care," but really, it was Netflix. Healing is a process, not perfection. And grace covers even the messy moments.

## A Reflection for You

- Am I practicing real self-care, or just surface-level comfort?
- Where am I still holding on to lies that keep me in the shadows?
- How can I lean into faith, even when I don't have all the answers?

## In Closing

Healing in the light isn't about having everything figured out. It's about showing up for yourself with honesty, practicing self-care that restores instead of masks, and leaning on faith when your own strength feels small.

Because the light doesn't erase your scars, it helps you see them for what they are: evidence that you've survived, that you're still standing, and that you are worthy of joy, love, and peace.

# Chapter 14

Faith in the Fire –
Trusting God in the middle of the storm

It is easy to talk about faith after the storm has passed. When the sun is shining again and you can look back and say, "Look what God brought me through." But what about when you are still in the fire? When the smoke is thick, the heat is unbearable, and you cannot see a way out? That is where faith becomes more than a word. It becomes your lifeline.

## When I Questioned God

I wish I could say my faith was always steady, but it wasn't. There were nights I prayed and it felt like my prayers hit the ceiling. There were mornings I opened my eyes and wondered why God would let me wake up to more pain. I asked Him, "Why me? Why this? Why now?"

My faith wavered a lot during the years I endured trauma. Sometimes I thought I was like, "when is this punishment going to be over." Other times I felt like I wasn't fulfilling my duties, like I wasn't good enough, like I didn't deserve better, even though I craved it in my bones.

Faith in the fire doesn't always sound like praise. Sometimes it sounds like tears. Sometimes it sounds like silence. Sometimes it sounds like anger. And do you know what? God can handle all of it. He is big enough for your questions, your doubts, and even your frustration.

## What Faith Really Looks Like

Faith in the fire is not about pretending you are okay. It is not about putting on a fake smile and quoting scriptures you don't even believe in that moment. Faith in the fire is simply choosing to hold on, even when your grip feels weak.

It is saying, "God, I don't understand this. I don't like this. But I trust that You are still with me." And He promises that He is. In Hebrews 13:5 (NIV), God says, "Never will I leave you; never will I forsake you."

That promise holds even in the fire.

## The Peace of His Presence

God's word also reminds us in Isaiah 26:3 (NIV), "You will keep in perfect peace those whose minds are steadfast, because they trust in you."

It is important that we keep our minds stayed on Him, even in our despair. Because God is sovereign. He has you, your present, and your future in His hands. Even when the fire feels endless, His presence is unshakable.

## My Experience of God in the Fire

I remember praying desperately for God to make a way out. When the moment finally came, I realized I was not prepared for the aftermath. The storm did not stop overnight. The fire left ashes everywhere. But looking back, I see how God gave me strength even when I thought I had none. He gave me just enough to get through the day. And then He gave me more for the next.

God did not always calm the storm immediately, but He calmed me in the storm.

## Humor in the Faith Walk

There were times when I would pray, "God, I need a sign," and then something small would happen, like finding a dollar in my coat pocket. I would laugh and say, "Okay Lord, not the sign I was asking for, but thank You anyway." Faith has a way of teaching you to find light even in the smallest moments.

## A Reflection for You

- Have I been honest with God about my doubts, fears, or anger?
- What small signs of His presence have I overlooked in the middle of my storm?
- How can I remind myself that faith is not about perfection, but about holding on?

## In Closing

Faith in the fire is not easy. It stretches you, tests you, and exposes the parts of you that feel fragile. But it also strengthens you in ways you will not see until later.

If you are still in the fire, know this: God has not left you. Even when you cannot see Him, He is there. Even when you cannot feel Him, He is holding you. And one day, you will look back at the ashes and realize you were never walking through them alone.

Because He meant it when He said, "Never will I leave you; never will I forsake you." And He will keep you in perfect peace when your mind stays on Him.

# Faith Anchor: Psalms in the Fire

When we are in the fire, it helps to know we are not the first to walk through it. The book of Psalms is full of raw, honest prayers written by people who knew despair, fear, and heartbreak. These verses remind us that we are allowed to cry out to God, to question, and to hope, sometimes all in the same breath.

Here are a few scriptures to carry with you in the fire, with reflections to hold them close:

Psalm 34:18 (NIV)

"The Lord is close to the brokenhearted and saves those who are crushed in spirit."

When your heart feels shattered, remember this: God is not far from you. He is right there, close enough to catch every tear.

Psalm 42:5 (NIV)

"Why, my soul, are you downcast? Why so disturbed within me? Put your hope in God, for I will yet praise him, my Savior and my God."

Sometimes faith looks like talking to yourself. Remind your soul of where your hope belongs. Even when you don't feel like praising, you can declare, "I will yet praise Him."

Psalm 91:1–2 (NIV)

"Whoever dwells in the shelter of the Most High will rest in the shadow of the Almighty. I will say of the Lord, 'He is my refuge and my fortress, my God, in whom I trust.'"

God is not just watching over you, He is covering you. His shadow is a shelter, His presence is a refuge, and His arms are a fortress. You are safe with Him.

Psalm 30:5 (NIV)

"Weeping may stay for the night, but rejoicing comes in the morning."

The night does not last forever. The fire does not burn forever. The storm does not rage forever. Hold on, because joy is coming.

## In Closing

Psalms remind us that faith is not about always being strong. It is about being honest with God and trusting that He is strong enough for both of you. Carry these scriptures with you in your darkest nights. Pray them out loud. Write them down. Whisper them when you feel weak.

Because His Word is not just ink on a page. It is life, peace, and strength when the fire feels like too much.

# Chapter 15

## The Role of Motherhood in Healing –
## The challenges and beauty of rising for your children.

Motherhood is one of the hardest and most beautiful parts of healing. It adds weight to the journey, but it also brings light into the darkest places. When you are a mother, you do not just rise for yourself. You rise for the little eyes that are watching you, the little hearts that are shaped by your choices, and the little souls that are depending on your strength.

There were days when I felt like I had nothing left to give. I was broken, tired, and unsure how I was going to move forward. Then I would look at my children, and in their faces I saw both the reason for my pain and the reason for my healing. They carried the impact of what I had gone through, but they also gave me the courage to keep going.

### The Pressure of Motherhood in Hard Seasons

Being a mother in the middle of struggle comes with guilt. You question every decision. You wonder if your children will ever recover from what they have seen or what they have endured. I used to ask myself, "Did I ruin them? Will they grow up and resent me? Will they ever know the strength it took for me to keep us moving?"

Children do not feel like the burden in those moments. The real burden is not having enough strength to carry yourself, yet still having to carry them too. That weight feels unbearable at times. But over time, I began to see something important. My children were not just watching my pain. They were also watching my resilience.

## Lessons Our Children Learn From Us

Children learn strength not from never seeing struggle, but from watching how you rise after the fall. They learn honesty when you tell them the truth about mistakes and healing. They learn faith when they see you praying through tears. They learn love when they see you choose peace instead of chaos.

One day, my daughter told me, "Mom, stop crying. We're not crying, so don't you cry." She said she was happy that I got them out, and in that moment, her strength became mine.

## Humor in Motherhood

Motherhood in healing also comes with those moments you can laugh about. Like the time I tried to have a "deep family talk" with my kids, pouring my heart out, and one of them interrupted to ask what was for dinner. In that moment I realized, healing is important, but so is pizza night. Kids have a way of reminding us not to take everything so seriously.

## A Reflection for You

- How has motherhood pushed me to rise, even when I felt like I could not?
- Am I giving myself grace as a mother, knowing my children do not need perfection, only presence?
- What lessons of healing and strength do I want my children to carry from watching me?

## In Closing

Motherhood can feel like both a burden and a blessing in the healing journey. But the truth is, it is one of the greatest motivators for rising. When you heal, you are not just breaking cycles for yourself. You are breaking them for the generations that follow.

Your children do not need a perfect mother. They need a present one. And when they see you rise, they will learn how to rise too.

# Chapter 16

## Breaking Generational Chains –
## Choosing to End Cycles and Begin Anew

Generational chains are the patterns, habits, and wounds that get passed down from one generation to the next. They may not always be obvious at first, but they shape how families think, live, and love. Some of these patterns are healthy, but many of them are destructive.

The truth is, breaking generational chains is not easy. It takes courage to stand up and say, "This stops with me."

## Realizing the Cycles

It can take time, experiences, wisdom, and maturity before you even realize what chains exist in your family. Sometimes it comes through hearing shared stories, noticing repeated patterns, or reflecting on your own struggles. You may not even see the cycle clearly until later in life when you finally connect the dots.

We all come from someone and somewhere. We all have history, whether it is beautiful, painful, or both. And it is not easy to break cycles that have been repeated for generations.

Breaking chains takes awareness, acceptance, a decision, prayer, and often fasting. We won't get into all of that too deeply here, because that could be a whole other book. But I want to have this conversation with you because it matters.

## Connected to Someone Else's Cycle

Sometimes the weight isn't just from your own family. You could be sharing your space, your time, or your life with someone else who is carrying serious generational cycles that need to be broken. You may find yourself questioning their behavior or decisions over and over again. Then, through a conversation with them, a family member, or someone who knows their background, you realize you are not just connected to the person. You are connected to their cycle.

I have experienced this firsthand in different areas of my life. It is draining, confusing, and painful to carry the weight of chains that were never yours to begin with. But that awareness is important, because it helps you decide how to move forward.

## The Hard Truth About Chains

Generational trauma doesn't just disappear because you want it to. It requires intention. Sometimes it requires counseling. Often it requires faith, prayer, and fasting. And always, it requires the courage to choose differently, even when it feels uncomfortable.

## Humor in the Healing

I remember one conversation with a family member where I pointed out how they handled something, and they shrugged and said, "That's just how we are." I laughed because for years I had accepted that excuse too. But the truth is, just because "that's how we are" doesn't mean that's how we have to stay.

## A Reflection for You

- What cycles or patterns have I seen in my family that I no longer want to repeat?
- Have I been carrying the weight of someone else's cycles?
- What steps can I take — spiritually, emotionally, or practically — to begin breaking chains?

## In Closing

Breaking generational chains is not easy, but it is possible. It takes honesty, prayer, and the willingness to step into a new way of living. And when you break those chains, you are not just doing it for yourself. You are doing it for your children, and for every generation that comes after you.

Your healing is not only personal. It is legacy.

# Part Four: Rising Strong

# Chapter 17

## Boundaries That Bless –
## Protecting Your Peace Without Apology

Let's get this straight: boundaries are not walls. They're not punishment. And they're not about shutting people out. Boundaries are doors with locks, you decide who has the key, who gets to enter, and how long they get to stay.

For too long, I thought setting boundaries made me mean, selfish, or "too much." I used to bend until I broke, then wonder why I felt resentful and exhausted. What I didn't realize was this: boundaries aren't about controlling other people. They're about protecting the peace God gave you.

## Why Boundaries Feel So Hard

We struggle with boundaries because we don't want to disappoint people. We fear being seen as "difficult" or "uncaring." And let's be real, some of us were taught that love means sacrifice, even if that sacrifice destroys us.

But here's the truth: if your "yes" is costing you your peace, your time, your health, or your joy, then it was never love in the first place. Boundaries don't ruin relationships; the lack of them does.

## My Boundary Wake-Up Call

I had so many moments when someone would ask me to do something, and deep down the voice inside me was screaming, "I really can't. I really don't want to." Not because I was trying to be mean, but because I truly needed to be in my own space, tending to my own moments.

But instead of listening to that inner voice, I'd smile and say yes. Outwardly agreeable, inwardly exhausted. And every time, I ended up frustrated — not at them, but at myself. Because I hadn't honored the boundary that was already inside me. I ignored the most powerful word I had at my disposal: no.

## Boundaries as Blessings

Here's the beauty of boundaries: they don't just protect you — they bless others too. When you're clear about your limits, people know how to treat you. When you protect your time and energy, you show up more fully present in the relationships that truly matter.

And boundaries also teach others that they are capable of taking responsibility for their own lives. Every time you say, "No, I can't do that," you're not abandoning them, you're giving them the opportunity to grow.

## Humor in the Boundaries

I used to think saying no required so much explanation. Like somehow my grown-woman self was going to "get in trouble" for saying no. I'd overthink it, imagining people talking about me, saying mean things, or questioning my reasons. And then I'd sit there rehearsing how I was going to justify myself, as if I needed permission to honor my own limits.

## A Reflection for You

- Where in my life am I saying yes out of guilt instead of love?
- Do I believe setting boundaries makes me selfish, or do I see them as self-respect?
- What's one boundary I can put in place today that will protect my peace?

## In Closing

Boundaries are not burdens. They are blessings. They keep you whole, present, and free to give love from a place of fullness instead of depletion.

So stop apologizing for the locks on your doors. Your peace is worth protecting, and the right people in your life will honor the key you've entrusted to them.

# Chapter 18

## The Courage to Let Go –
## Releasing What Is Unworthy of Your Presence

Letting go sounds simple until it's your turn to do it.

We love to talk about moving on, releasing, and "choosing ourselves," but when it's time to actually walk away, it feels like pulling your own heart out of your chest. That's because letting go isn't just a decision...it's an act of courage. And courage always costs something.

## Why Letting Go Feels Impossible

There are a few reasons we cling to things that no longer serve us:

- Familiarity: Even pain can feel comfortable when it's all you've known.
- Fear: What if I never find anything better? What if I end up alone?
- Fantasy: We don't let go of the person, we let go of the dream of what they might become.
- Guilt: We feel responsible for someone else's happiness, even at the expense of our own.

I've been there, holding on to someone I should've released long before, convincing myself that my presence could save them. But here's the truth: you cannot save someone who is determined to stay broken.

## My Own Letting-Go Moment

There came a point where I had to face reality: I was losing myself while trying to hold on to someone unworthy of my presence. And the hardest part wasn't leaving them, it was letting go of the version of me who thought staying was strength.

I remember sitting with that realization, feeling grief and relief at the same time. Grief because I mourned what I thought my life would be, and relief because deep down I knew I deserved more. Letting go didn't feel like winning, it felt like dying to the version of myself that had been okay with less.

## The Quiet Courage of Release

Courage isn't always loud. Sometimes it's quiet, packing your things while praying for God to hold you together. Sometimes it's choosing silence instead of another exhausting argument. Sometimes it's waking up one morning and deciding, "I can't live like this anymore."

Letting go isn't weakness. It's strength that whispers, "Enough."

## Humor in the Letting Go

I remember blocking someone on social media and making sure I blocked every account I believed was theirs. I thought I had finally shut another door. Only for them to create another account just to say, "Hey."

That moment made me laugh because it showed me something important: letting go doesn't mean people will stop reaching for you, it means you've finally stopped reaching back.

## A Reflection for You

- What am I still holding on to that no longer deserves space in my life?
- Am I clinging to the person, or to the dream I built around them?
- What could open up if I had the courage to let go?

## In Closing

Letting go is never easy. It takes faith, courage, and trust that what you're walking toward is greater than what you're walking away from.

And here's the promise I can make: every time you release what is unworthy of your presence, you make room for what is worthy. You create space for peace, joy, and love that doesn't break you but lifts you higher.

Because courage isn't about holding on the longest. Courage is about knowing when to let go.

# Chapter 19

## Love That Lifts –
## Redefining Love as Healing, Whole, and Holy

When I was younger, my thought of love was simple: peaceful, no disagreements, every day like ice cream and sunny skies. And of course, once children came along, they'd be perfect too. I know, right? What a delusion. That was my childhood idea of love.

But as I matured and gained life experience, I discovered the truth; that even in real love there are disagreements, hardships, sick days, vacation days, days when all you want is to be wrapped in your lover's arms, and times when you need space to breathe. Not because you don't love them or want them near, but because we're human, and sometimes we need time alone to reflect, to meditate, to just be.

Even though I discovered this later in life, my own love life didn't always reflect that understanding. The love I knew was heavy, sometimes unbearable. It broke me down, ate away at my spirit, and left me depleted, and unsure where I'd find the strength to refill so I could keep showing up, not just for myself, but for my children.

Love that lifts doesn't silence you, it gives your voice space. It doesn't break you down, it builds you up. It doesn't drain you, it pours into you. Love isn't supposed to feel like chains, it's supposed to feel like wings. Real love lifts.

## What Love Is Not

Let's be clear. Love is not:

- Control disguised as protection.
- Pain justified by apologies.
- Red flags turned green with excuses.
- Silence in the name of peace.

That's not love, that's survival dressed up as commitment.

## What Love Can Be

Love at its best is healing, whole, and holy. It's the kind of love that:

- Calls out the best in you without dimming your light.
- Honors your boundaries instead of testing them.
- Feels safe enough for you to be vulnerable and strong at the same time.
- Doesn't compete with your relationship with God, but draws you closer to Him.

Love that lifts doesn't make you fall apart, it helps you rise into who you were created to be.

## My First Glimpse of Lifting Love

After over 24 years of toxic cycles, I didn't know what healthy love even looked like. I was so used to chaos that calm felt suspicious. I'd catch myself waiting for an explosion that never came. Slowly, I began to realize that love wasn't supposed to be a rollercoaster. It was supposed to feel consistent.

I remember the first time someone respected a boundary I set. It startled me. I thought, "Wait… you're not mad? You're not going to punish me for saying no?" That moment was small, but it was revolutionary. It showed me that love can lift by simply allowing you to be yourself without fear.

## Humor in Redefining Love

I'll admit, learning what real love looks like was awkward at first. It felt like trying on new shoes and not knowing how to walk in them. I kept waiting for the pinch, the blister, the hurt, and when it didn't come, I didn't know what to do with myself. It's funny how peace can feel strange when all you've ever known is chaos.

## A Reflection for You

- Have I mistaken survival for love in my past?
- What would it look like to experience love that lifts instead of drains?
- Do I believe I'm worthy of a love that is healing, whole, and holy?

## In Closing

Love that lifts is not perfect, but it is possible. It's patient, it's safe, it's kind and it's not just something you wait to receive from someone else. It begins within you.

The more you honor yourself, walk in truth, and embrace healing, the more you'll recognize real love when it arrives. Because love that lifts will never ask you to fall. It will rise with you.

# Chapter 20

Rediscovering You –
Finding laughter, identity, and joy after loss.

When you've spent years surviving, it's easy to forget who you are outside of the struggle. You get so caught up in carrying weight, putting out fires, and holding everyone else together, that when the dust finally settles, you don't even recognize yourself.

Rediscovering yourself after loss feels strange at first. You almost don't trust the quiet. You wonder if it's safe to laugh, to dream, to enjoy life again. But this part of the journey is sacred, because it's where you remember that you are more than what you've been through.

## Who Am I Without the Pain?

I had to ask myself that question many times. Who am I when I'm not fighting to survive? Who am I when I'm not someone's wife, fixer, or rescuer? Who am I when the chaos is gone?

The truth is, you don't lose yourself forever. She's still there, waiting for you to invite her back. Sometimes she shows up in small moments, singing in the car, enjoying a meal without rushing, laughing so hard your stomach hurts.

## The Gift of Laughter

One day, some time after leaving, I cried so hard, so hard it turned into laughter. Sounds strange, right? But in that moment, my tears turned into laughter because I thought, "Girl, look at you, you did that." I realized I was on my road of freedom, and the load didn't feel as heavy anymore.

Laughter is medicine. It doesn't erase the scars, but it reminds you that your spirit is still alive and capable of joy. Every laugh is proof that healing is happening, even if you don't notice it right away.

## Identity Beyond the Roles

Rediscovering you also means finding your identity outside of roles. You are more than someone's mother, daughter, partner, or employee. You are a woman with passions, talents, and dreams.

For me, rediscovery came slowly. I started trying new things, reconnecting with old hobbies, even saying yes to little adventures that reminded me I was still here. It wasn't about proving anything. It was about giving myself permission to live.

## Humor in Rediscovery

I'll admit, rediscovery can feel awkward. Like the time I decided to "reclaim my joy" by going roller skating again… and let's just say my knees reminded me that I wasn't sixteen anymore. Still, I laughed, and that laughter reminded me that even falling on the floor felt better than falling back into who I used to be.

## A Reflection for You

- What makes me laugh so hard that I forget my pain, even for a moment?

- Who am I outside of the roles I play for others?

- What small steps can I take to rediscover myself today?

## In Closing

Rediscovering yourself is not about erasing the past. It's about reclaiming your joy, your identity, and your right to live fully.

You are not only the woman who survived. You are the woman who laughs again, who dreams again, who rediscovers her beauty, strength, and light.

It's about remembering who you were all along, and how much of a better woman you are now, and will continue to be, because of the wisdom you now hold.

Because healing isn't just about letting go of what broke you. It's about rising into the woman you were always meant to become.

# Couch Talk: Let's Talk About Rest

Sis, can we be honest? Rest is hard when you've lived in survival mode.

When you've spent years walking on eggshells, always on alert, always "on," rest doesn't feel natural. It feels unsafe. You catch yourself waiting for something bad to happen the moment you let your guard down.

But here's the truth: rest is not a luxury. Rest is healing.

## Why Rest Feels So Strange

When I finally found myself free, I realized I didn't even know how to relax. I would sit down on the couch, and my mind would start racing with all the things I "should" be doing. Laundry. Work. Cleaning. Planning. Anything but sitting still.

It took time for me to understand that busyness had become my coping mechanism. If I kept moving, I didn't have to feel. And if I didn't feel, maybe I wouldn't hurt. But healing requires stillness, and stillness requires rest.

## Rest as a Form of Trust

Rest is also spiritual. Every time you rest, you're saying, "God, I trust You enough to stop striving." That's why He gave us the Sabbath — not to put another rule on us, but to give us a rhythm of restoration.

And here's the thing: sometimes rest looks like a nap, sometimes it looks like saying no, and sometimes it looks like laughing with friends. Rest doesn't have to be complicated. It just has to give your body, mind, and spirit a chance to breathe.

## Reflection for You

- Do I feel guilty when I rest, as if I'm doing something wrong?

- What keeps me from allowing myself to slow down?

- How can I practice rest this week, even if only in small ways?

## In Closing

Rest is not laziness. Rest is strength. It is the quiet place where God refills your cup and reminds you that you don't have to carry everything on your own.

So give yourself permission to pause. To breathe. To rest. You deserve it.

# Chapter 21

Love and Friendship – The healing power of
sisterhood, support, and community.

Healing is often painted as a solo journey, but the truth is, we are not built
to do it alone. Yes, there are parts of the process that are deeply personal,
but there is also a kind of strength that only comes from walking with
others who understand, encourage, and remind you of who you are when
you forget.

Sisterhood, family, friendship, and community are lifelines. They remind
us that we are not the only ones carrying scars, and that healing becomes
lighter when it is shared.

## Why We Need Each Other

When you've been through trauma or loss, isolation feels natural. You
convince yourself no one will understand, or worse, that people will judge
you if they know the truth. But isolation only feeds shame.

Real community does the opposite. It shines light on your story and says,
"Me too." It tells you that you're not crazy, not weak, not alone. And
sometimes, those simple words are enough to keep you moving forward.

## My Experience With Sisterhood and Family

I will never forget the nights I sat with women who had walked through their own storms. We cried together, but we also laughed until our sides hurt. We prayed for one another, lifted each other up, and sometimes just sat in silence when words weren't enough.

But it wasn't just my sisters in spirit who carried me. My family played a major part in my healing too. I know that without their support, I would not have made it. Some of them had no idea of the trauma and damage that had been done, but even in their not knowing, they still tried to understand. They still loved me unconditionally. They still showed up for me and for my children.

That love became an anchor when everything else felt unsteady. It reminded me that even when the people I trusted most had broken me, there were others who were willing to stand in the gap, hold space for me, and love me back to life.

## Humor in Friendship and Family

Support in healing isn't always deep talks and tears. Sometimes it's laughing over something silly that has nothing to do with your pain. Sometimes it's inside jokes that no one else would get. Sometimes it's being able to sit in sweatpants with no makeup on and knowing you're loved exactly as you are.

And if you have family, you know sometimes their love shows up in the simplest ways. Like a hot meal, watching the kids so you can breathe, or just saying, "Come sit with us, you don't have to explain." Those little moments are proof that love is healing too.

## A Reflection for You

- Do I have safe people in my life who I can be fully myself with?

- Have I been isolating myself when what I really need is community?

- Who are the sisters, friends, or family I can lean on in this season of healing?

## In Closing

Love, family, and friendship are powerful parts of the healing journey. They don't take away the scars, but they remind you that you don't have to carry the weight alone.

Community gives you courage. Sisterhood gives you strength. Family gives you stability. Friendship gives you joy.

Because healing is not just about rediscovering yourself. It is also about rediscovering the beauty of walking with others who help you rise.

# Part Five: A Legacy of Love

# Chapter 22

Rising for the Next Generation – How Your Healing
Impacts Your Children and Future Family

Your healing is not just about you. It's about the people who are watching
you, learning from you, and being shaped by the choices you make. When
you rise, you give the next generation permission to rise too.

## They Are Watching You

Children, nieces, nephews, younger cousins, even the young women
around you, they are all watching. They see how you respond to pain,
how you set boundaries, how you carry yourself, and how you love.

When I was in the middle of my trauma, I worried every day about what
my kids were absorbing. Were they learning dysfunction instead of peace?
Fear instead of faith? But then I realized something. They weren't just
watching my pain. They were watching my healing. They were seeing me
cry, pray, and still get back up. And that taught them resilience.

## Breaking What Could Have Continued

We often say we want to give our children "better." But better isn't always
about money, houses, or opportunities. Sometimes "better" is simply
breaking cycles. Better is showing them what healthy love looks like.
Better is teaching them how to rest, laugh, forgive, and trust God.

Healing means the next generation doesn't have to carry the same chains. They can build on your strength instead of repeating your wounds.

## A Personal Moment

One time when I left, one of my daughters looked at me and said, "Mom, I'm proud of you." Those words melted my heart. They made me feel good in a way I can't fully explain. Because even though my decisions had caused a lot of chaos, she saw that I was physically making the effort to not only free myself, but to free them too. She saw action over words. She saw me trying to break from the old and from what was not working. She saw that I was truly rooting for peace.

## Humor in the Legacy

I've had some hiccups at times when trying to set boundaries, and my kids definitely don't have a problem pointing those hiccups out to me. Out of the mouths of babes, right? They have a way of keeping me honest, reminding me that I'm still learning too.

## Reflection for You

- What cycles do I want to make sure my children or the next generation don't repeat?
- Am I showing them not just survival, but joy and peace?
- How can I be more intentional about rising for them, even while I'm still rising for myself?

## In Closing

Rising for the next generation is legacy work. It means you are planting seeds of healing, wisdom, and faith that will outlive you. It means your scars become their strength, your choices become their freedom, and your story becomes their testimony of what is possible.

Your healing is not only saving you. It is shaping the future.

# Chapter 23

## Rising in Community – Using Your Healing to Serve, Lead, and Uplift Others

Sis, your healing isn't just for you. It's also for the people God will send across your path. Every scar, every tear, every lesson becomes part of the way you love and serve others. Healing gives you compassion for pain you recognize, and wisdom for struggles you've already walked through.

### The Ripple Effect of Healing

Think about it. When you walk into a room carrying peace, you shift the atmosphere. When you speak truth with love, you plant seeds in someone else's life. When you share your story, even just a little, it can give another woman the courage to speak up about hers.

You don't have to be standing on a stage or leading a movement for your healing to matter. Sometimes rising in community looks like listening without judgment, offering a prayer, or simply being a safe place for someone who feels alone.

## My Own Experience

When I started sharing pieces of my journey, I was nervous. I wondered if people would look at me differently, or worse, judge me. But what I found was the opposite. Women leaned in. They said, "Me too." They told me about their pain, their struggles, and their own scars. And in those conversations, I realized that community is built on honesty, not perfection.

Your vulnerability becomes someone else's lifeline.

## The Call to Serve

Healing equips you to lead, not because you have it all together, but because you've walked through the fire and survived. You carry empathy where others might carry judgment. You know how to sit with someone in their pain without needing to fix them. And you know how to remind them that rising is possible, because you're living proof.

Serving and leading doesn't always mean doing something big. It means being faithful with what's in front of you. It means showing up for your community, your church, your workplace, or your sisters with love and wisdom.

And as you do, remember to give grace. The same way God has poured grace into your life, pour that grace into others. Not everyone has the tools, support, or love that you may have had when you needed it. Some are still searching. Some are still stumbling. Grace makes room for them to grow.

And don't forget to give that same grace to yourself. Healing is a process, not a straight line.

## Humor in Community

I used to think "uplifting others" meant I had to talk, or that someone else had to say something. Later, I found that uplifting someone could mean sitting quietly next to them, giving them a tissue as tears roll down their cheeks, sitting at your friend's house with your feet propped up watching a great show, or simply making someone a good cup of tea or coffee. Sometimes, it's just that simple.

## Reflection for You

- How has my healing shaped the way I see others in pain?
- Where in my community can I show up as a safe place for someone else?
- Am I willing to let my story, even the painful parts, become part of how I serve?
- Am I extending grace to others and to myself the same way God has extended it to me?

## In Closing

Rising in community doesn't require perfection. It requires presence. It requires honesty. It requires a willingness to use your healing to help others rise too.

Because when you rise, you light the way for someone else. And when we rise together, we are unstoppable.

# Chapter 24

She Rises Forward –

You were never meant to fall, you were meant to rise.

If you've made it this far, I want you to take a deep breath. Really, pause and breathe. Feel your chest rise. Feel your lungs fill with air. That breath is proof that you are still here, still moving, still rising.

This book has not been about perfection. It has not been about pretending the past never happened. It has been about facing truth, grieving what was lost, peeling back the layers, and rediscovering the strength and beauty that was always inside you.

You were never meant to fall. Not in love, not in life, not in spirit. You were meant to rise.

## Rising is a Choice

Rising doesn't mean life will be easy from here. You will still face challenges, moments of doubt, days when the weight feels heavy. But rising is a choice you make again and again. It is the decision to get back up when life knocks you down. It is the courage to believe that your story is not over.

Rising is choosing healing over hiding. It is choosing joy over fear. It is choosing to love yourself enough to walk away from what no longer serves you, and to walk toward what makes you whole.

## Your Scars Are Not the End

Every scar you carry tells a story. Not of defeat, but of survival. Not of weakness, but of strength. You may have been broken, but you are not destroyed. You may have been bruised, but you are not bound.

Some years ago, I had a saying: "Prayerfully made, beautifully scarred." That still holds true to this day. Once I came to grips with the trauma I experienced, I realized that no matter what I had been through, my scars were beautiful. They were beautiful because I grew from them. They were beautiful because I gained wisdom. They were beautiful because I learned to rise in love with every part of me, even the parts that did not experience better.

Your scars are the proof that you fell and got back up again. They are the evidence that you are rising.

## Moving Forward Together

As you step forward, I want you to know this: you are not alone. Even when you feel isolated, even when no one else seems to understand, there are women just like you, sisters who have carried pain and found hope again. We are rising together.

And when you forget your strength, remember this moment. Remember this truth. Remember that you were never meant to fall, you were always meant to rise.

## Closing Words

My prayer for you is that you will leave this book not only encouraged, but empowered. That you will walk forward knowing you have the tools to protect your peace, embrace your worth, and welcome love that lifts you instead of breaks you.

You are more than your past. You are more than your scars. You are a woman rising in love, rising in truth, and rising in strength.

Prayerfully made. Beautifully scarred. Wonderfully rising.

And this, my dear sister, is only the beginning.

My Dear Sisters,

If you are holding this book in your hands right now, I want you to know something: you are not alone.

I know what it feels like to cry silently behind closed doors while smiling in front of everyone else. I know what it feels like to pray for change, to crave freedom in your bones, and to wonder if you will ever truly be whole again. I know what it feels like to look at your scars and question if they mean you are damaged goods.

But I also know this: you are still here. And because you are still here, there is still hope.

Your journey may not look like mine, but pain is universal. Trauma may have touched your life through love, family, friendships, strangers, or even work, but the healing process belongs to you. And with every step forward, you are rewriting your story.

I want you to remember this truth: scars do not make you ugly, weak, or unworthy. They are the evidence that you fought battles and survived. They are the proof that you grew, that you learned, that you are wiser and stronger than you realize.

You were prayerfully made. You are beautifully scarred. And you are worthy of love, joy, peace, and freedom.

So walk forward knowing you do not rise alone. We are rising together - as sisters, as women, as daughters of a God who promises, "Never will I leave you; never will I forsake you." He has you. He has your present. He has your future.

This is not the end of your story. It is the beginning of a new chapter. And I am honored that we got to walk through these pages together.

With love,

J. Renee'

# Chapter 26

Affirmations for Rising –
10 short affirmations to carry in everyday life.

- I remind myself that I am worthy of love that lifts me higher, not love that drags me down.
- I carry this truth: my scars are not shame, they are proof that I survived and I am still standing.
- I choose peace over chaos, and joy over fear, even when it feels uncomfortable at first.
- I tell myself daily that the cycles I came from do not define the woman I am becoming.
- I give myself grace by forgiving what I did not know then, and honoring who I am now.
- I remind myself that boundaries are a form of love, and I can say no without apology.
- I hold on to God's promise: He will never leave me, nor forsake me, no matter what season I face.
- I release what is unworthy of my presence, and I create room for what is good and true.
- I laugh, I rest, I breathe, because joy is healing and I deserve it.
- I carry this with me: I am wiser, stronger, and rising forward in love every single day.

# Chapter 27

A Prayer for the Journey –
Closing in faith, hope, and love.

Heavenly Father,

I thank You for my sister who has walked through these pages. I thank You for her heart, her courage, her scars, and her desire to rise. Lord, You know her story in ways no one else ever could. You know every tear she has cried, every burden she has carried, and every prayer she has whispered in the dark.

Today, I lift her to You. Surround her with Your perfect love. Remind her of Your promise in Hebrews 13:5 that You will never leave her, nor forsake her. Keep her mind stayed on You so that she may rest in Your perfect peace, just as You promised in Isaiah 26:3.

Father, I ask that You continue to heal every place that feels broken. Restore her joy, renew her strength, and show her that her scars are not the end of her story. They are the evidence of Your power and her resilience. Let her know deep in her soul that she is prayerfully made and beautifully scarred, and that her future rests safely in Your hands.

Give her courage to set boundaries, wisdom to make choices that honor her worth, and faith to trust You even in the fire. And when she forgets how strong she is, remind her that she is never rising alone. You are with her, and so are the sisters walking beside her in spirit.

Lord, I pray that her life will be a testimony of hope, healing, and love that lifts. May she rise forward, not in her own strength, but in Yours.

In Jesus' name, Amen.

FOR ADDITIONAL BOOKS OR TO SCHEDULE THE AUTHOR
FOR SPEAKING
ENGAGEMENTS, CONTACT:
EMAIL: love11thhr@gmail.com
WEBSITE: www.loveatthe11thhour.com